POEMS

"A biography-in-verse that brims with beauty, pain, insight, and humility, *Thérèse* informs as it inspires. In Sarah Law's honest and perceptive portrayals, the 'busy stillness' and 'little ways' of this Carmelite nun become a 'petal, flaming high in Christ's kaleidoscope.' This is a poetry pilgrimage you'll want to take."

—**Marjorie Maddox,** author of *Transplant, Transport, Transubstantiation*

"Little souls, little petals, little Carmelite—the word *little* is intrinsically woven into the life of St. Thérèse of Lisieux, and it appears repeatedly, in all the right places, in this poetic biography of the saint. The poems enthrall by their attention to sensory detail and the underlying strength they evince. Through them we learn how Thérèse's 'little world blossom[ed] / under her sword's steel.' A deeply moving and memorable work."

—**Sofia Starnes,** author of *The Consequence of Moonlight: Poems*

"In lyrical snapshots Sarah Law has captured the most important events in the short life of the Carmelite whom Pope Pius X called 'the greatest saint of modern times.' *I will come back*, she promised, and these powerful poems make her real, present, accessible: 'she will be your sister, / with a shield, and a sword, / a rose, / and a whispered word.'"

—**Robert J. Edmonson, CJ,** translator of *The Complete Thérèse of Lisieux*

"Thérèse of Lisieux had the soul of a poet, and this life of Thérèse in poetry, inspired by the photos, reminiscences, and incidents of the saint, penetrates the depths hidden in the seeming triviality of her life and her 'resolute littleness,' adding fresh and new insight."

—**Jennifer Moorcroft,** author of *Saint Thérèse of Lisieux and her Sisters*

THÉRÈSE

POEMS

SARAH LAW

PARACLETE PRESS
BREWSTER, MASSACHUSETTS

2020 First Printing

Thérèse: Poems

Copyright © 2020 by Sarah Law

ISBN 978-1-64060-394-3

The Paraclete Press name and logo (dove on cross) are trademarks of Paraclete Press, Inc.

    Library of Congress Cataloging-in-Publication Data
Names: Law, Sarah, 1967- author.
Title: Thérèse : poems / Sarah Law.
Description: Brewster, Massachusetts : Paraclete Press, 2020. | Includes
  bibliographical references. | Summary: "Law uses poetry to gain insight
  into St. Therese's life and the conclusion that 'Everything is Grace'"--
  Provided by publisher.
Identifiers: LCCN 2020014693 (print) | LCCN 2020014694 (ebook) | ISBN
  9781640603943 | ISBN 9781640603950 (mobi) | ISBN 9781640603967 (epub) |
  ISBN 9781640603974 (pdf)
Subjects: LCSH: Thérèse, de Lisieux, Saint, 1873-1897--Poetry. | LCGFT:
  Poetry.
Classification: LCC PR6062.A842 T47 2020 (print) | LCC PR6062.A842
  (ebook) | DDC 821/.914--dc23
LC record available at https://lccn.loc.gov/2020014693
LC ebook record available at https://lccn.loc.gov/2020014694

10 9 8 7 6 5 4 3 2 1

Published by Paraclete Press
Brewster, Massachusetts
www.paracletepress.com

Printed in the United States of America

CONTENTS

AFTERWARDS

Introduction

owards the end of her short life, a twenty-four-year-old woman came to the conclusion that 'Everything is grace.' Sister Thérèse had received little education and seen little of the world, and she died before the start of the twentieth century. But something about, or within, her life had led her to this lucid insight. It is difficult to identify exactly what qualities have made her such a significant figure for many, including me. This elusive quality of grace she both perceived and embodied has drawn me back over many years (far more years of life than Thérèse had herself) to look again at her life in all its resonant littleness. And because resonant littleness is such a hallmark of her life and spirituality, it seemed appropriate for me to approach Thérèse with poetry, a form that often works with littleness as a way of approaching mystery.

Marie Françoise-Thérèse Martin was born in 1873, in Alençon, Normandy, the final child and fifth surviving daughter of Louis and Zélie Martin, devout Catholics and members of the bourgeois middle class. Thérèse's mother died when Thérèse was four. Louis moved the family to Lisieux to be nearer to his brother-in-law, Isidore Guérin, and his family. Thérèse briefly attended school but was mostly home educated. When she was nine, Thérèse's favourite older sister, Pauline, left for the Carmelite convent in Lisieux. Four years later, her eldest sister, Marie, joined the same convent. Two years after that in 1888 Thérèse herself entered the Carmel at the age of fifteen. Her sister Céline joined the same convent in 1894 after the death of their father, bringing her camera with her.

Thérèse was an obedient, affectionate, and attentive nun. In the Carmel she developed a spirituality that was notably confident and daring rather than fearful. Her 'little way' also emphasises the value of small acts done with love and thereby imbued with meaning. She died tragically young, after months of dreadful suffering, from tuberculosis in September 1897. Because of the spiritual value placed on reparatory suffering prevalent in nineteenth-century French Catholicism, she was denied significant pain relief in these last agonising weeks. She also struggled with doubts about the existence of heaven throughout these last months of her life, finding consolation in neither faith nor hope. But within the confines of her circumstances, her will was extremely strong, and her commitment to love God and her religious sisters was remarkable. So too was her wider love for humanity and the sense she had, towards the end of her life, that after death she would continue her mission to help those on earth. However, at her death, another nun in the same community wondered whatever could be said about Thérèse, the young sister who had been so kind and quiet. Surely her obituary would be extremely brief?

In fact, her death-notice or *circulaire*, an obituary circulated among other Carmelite convents, was comprised of Thérèse's own writings, and was in effect a book-length memoir. It was found so moving that when it became available to the general public, further print-runs were needed. By 1925 Thérèse was canonised and declared 'the greatest saint of modern times' by Pope Saint Pius X. In 1997 she was proclaimed a Doctor of the Church. She is Patroness of the Missions, of France, of Russia, and of florists. Her relics have toured the world. Even in the twenty-first century, she is immensely popular among devout Catholics and beyond. In 2009 thousands of people came to pay respects to her relics when they visited various venues in England; in 2019 they visited Scotland. They have toured much of the rest of the world too. There is something about Thérèse which still catches at the heart.

Her memoir has never been out of print and has been translated into many languages. As well as the three manuscripts which make up *The Story of a Soul* and Thérèse's own letters, poems and short plays, there are her purported last words recorded by her sisters, family correspondence, and witness statements for the beatification and canonisation processes. As one reads these, certain moments in Thérèse's life stand out as lucid and resonant, if not conventionally significant, and from these moments I drew many of my poems. For example, when she was a very young child, she wanted to know how everyone could be filled with God's love when so many were small and far from perfect: her older sister Pauline poured water into a tall glass and a little cup to show her that neither was fuller than the other. Another example is the 'conversion' from tearful sensitivity she felt one Christmas as a teenager. She prayed for Henri Pranzini, a condemned criminal, and was convinced that she had been given a sign of his conversion on the scaffold. Telling her beloved father she wanted to enter the Carmel, she was moved when he picked and gave her a little white flower. Then there is the daring spiritual metaphor she drew from her experience of being in a lift, or elevator, during her 1887 trip to Paris: she likened it to the undeserved uplift of divine love. Also in 1887 she begged Pope Leo XIII for permission to become a Carmelite, having been told by the Bishop that she was too young. Pauline (then Sister Agnès) tried to console her in her struggle to have her vocation recognised by suggesting she was an abandoned plaything of the child Jesus—a somewhat bittersweet analogy.

When she entered Carmel, at the age of just fifteen, the strict rules and enclosed lifestyle meant that Sister Thérèse of the Child

Jesus and of the the Holy Face (her chosen names) had to find ways of loving others and of understanding herself through further instances of littleness: of helping an elderly sister to the refectory; accepting another sister's irritating noises during prayer; finding peace and grace in chores as much as community worship, writing her poems, plays, letters, and memoir in scraps of free time, and finally enduring the physical and mental anguish of her last months. She also directed, unoffically, a small group of novices, and she wrote to a missionary priest and a seminarian, the latter of whom revealed his own fears and doubts to her. Had she been a man, she said, she would have become a priest herself. But instead she chose to become Love itself at the heart of the Church.

Perhaps the most poignant mementos of Thérèse's brief life are the photographic ones. Forty-seven photographic images survive, the early ones taken in a Lisieux photography studio. Most of them subsequent to her becoming a Carmelite were taken by Thérèse's sister Céline, including two taken after Thérèse's death. Sepia-tinted, surprisingly detailed, these photographs are all available online (at the Archives of the Carmel of Lisieux). The Darlot lens used by Céline with her box-and-tripod camera required a nine-second exposure, so while some of her photographs are perfectly posed, others are a little blurry, enhancing the candid nature of their images. They are a glimpse into a hidden world: the nuns make hay, pummel laundry, sit in meditation, make altar breads, sew during recreation. Several photographs show Thérèse playing the part of Joan of Arc, a figure she greatly admired for her active and enduring faith. One of those images fell into the hands of publicity-seeking atheist Léo Taxil, who mocked it at a Parisian meeting held in 1897, a few months before Thérèse's death. Thérèse had sent it in friendship to a fictitious young woman fabricated by Taxil.

I found the photographs fascinating and at times very moving, and poetry inspired by several of them are woven throughout this collection, although the poems themselves are not dependent for interpretation upon their photographic source. And so this collection gradually came together. For all my reading and thinking about Thérèse, I don't pretend fully to represent or understand her, but to provide glimpses of her life, especially as they have affected me. I don't pretend to understand the depths of her final suffering, or the Prioress's unwillingness to alleviate it, and some of the poems do not shy away from this. But it does not seem to me that her life and death were for nothing.

Thérèse is present in the world as a much-loved saint, and she has also appeared in contemporary poetry, although not so prominently as other saints and mystics—perhaps because her life is lacking elements of the obviously wondrous or miraculous. She features in thoughtful individual poems by Rowan Williams, Mary Ruefle, and others. She has been referenced in contemporary fiction too, particularly Ron Hansen's 1991 novel *Mariette in Ecstasy*, and Michelle Roberts's 1992 *Daughters of the House*. Thérèse has also been poignantly represented in film and play, with Alain Cavalier's *Thérèse* (1986) and Michel Pascal's 2009 one-woman play *The Story of a Soul* (which was filmed in the Lisieux Carmel with Eva Hernandez) as prime examples.

Thérèse of Lisieux is a great saint indissolubly linked with littleness, in which, when leavened by love, she found great strength. I have tried to respond to Thérèse in the 'little' medium of poetry, which for me is a way to reflect on and share her life, her resolve, and her grace.

I was very much inspired by the wonderful archive material, including photographs, biographies, primary texts, letters, and

13

other information at the archive web pages of the Carmel of Lisieux. I write as a poet and not as a theologian, biographer, or spiritual advisor. There are many who do this much better than I could. I've included a short additional bibliography at the end of this collection, for those interested. I've also included a brief note directly below on the other characters mentioned in these poems.

BRIEF NOTES ON OTHER FIGURES MENTIONED

Rose Taillé: the peasant wet nurse who enabled Thérèse to thrive as a baby.

Zélie Martin (Mama): Thérèse's mother, who died of breast cancer when Thérèse was four.

Madame Besnier: a photographer in Lisieux.

Louis Martin (Papa): Thérèse's father, who developed dementia and died in 1894.

Pauline, also Mère (Mother) Agnès of Jesus: Thérèse's second-eldest sister, a substitute mother after Zélie's death. She entered the Carmelite Convent in 1882.

Marie, also Sister Marie of the Sacred Heart: Thérèse's eldest sister, who became a Carmelite nun in 1886.

Léonie, later Sister Marie-Françoise of the Convent of the Visitation: Thérèse's sister, troubled and difficult; older than Thérèse by ten years.

Céline, also Sister Geneviève of the Holy Face: Thérèse's sister, older than Thérèse by four years. Artistic, strong-willed, she entered Carmel in 1894, and, unusually, brought her camera with her.

Pierre Mabille: a twentieth-century surrealist writer who criticised Thérèse as a hysteric.

Henri Pranzini: a notorious convicted murderer. Thérèse prayed for his conversion. He unexpectedly kissed the crucifix before his execution in 1887.

INTRODUCTION

Jeanne Fleuriot: daughter of the property owner next to the Lisieux Carmel.

Sister Marie of the Trinity: a young novice, near in age to, and beloved by, Thérèse.

Sister Marie of the Eucharist ('Cousin Marie'): Marie Guérin, Thérèse's cousin.

Mère (Mother) Marie de Gonzague: Prioress of the Carmel of Lisieux; aristocratic, authoritarian, and temperamental.

Sister Marie-Madeleine of the Holy Sacrament: a novice, of nervous disposition.

Sister Martha: a novice, older and less spiritually able than Thérèse.

Sister Saint Peter: an elderly nun at the Carmel of Lisieux.

Sister Marie-Joseph: a nun at the Carmel of Lisieux, little liked.

Venerable Anne of Jesus: a contemporary of St Teresa of Avila, she brought the Carmelite Order to France in the early seventeenth century.

Diana Vaughan: a young female character fabricated by atheist Léo Taxil. He claimed Diana had escaped from an abusive Masonic cult and had subsequently converted to Catholicism, writing letters and testimonies in her name. The real Diana Vaughan was actually Taxil's middle-aged secretary.

Léo Taxil: an antagonistic atheist who tricked Catholic believers into thinking Diana Vaughan was a real person. He revealed his hoax in April 1897. Thérèse had sent 'Diana' a holy card featuring an image of herself as Joan of Arc. Taxil mockingly displayed the image during the public revelation of his hoax.

Dr. de Cornière: Doctor to the Lisieux Carmel.

L'Abbé (Father) Roulland: a missionary priest who corresponded with Thérèse.

L'Abbé (Father) Bellière (the unnamed seminarian in 'Brother'): a seminarian and later a missionary priest who corresponded with Thérèse, confessing his own temptations and weakness.

LOURDES COURTYARD

They come and go –
the holy souls,
to quench their thirst
in its bright water

and in this little square
where greenery courts
the dry chapel walls
a brief sunlight

finds her there,
absent and present,
sitting, hands in prayer
then standing back

by the window ledge
as though she is part
of the sun's course, its
moving, weightless pressure,

its fleeting warmth.
Close your eyes.
It is a busy stillness,
all bees and honeysuckle.

CHILDHOOD

Photo 1 *July 1876*

She has already lost one mother
– Rose Taillé the wet-nurse
in her white-walled cottage,

who loved Thérèse to life –
whose strong sap infused her
with a taste for iron and fire.

Soon she will lose another:
Zélie, the strict, the suffering,
whose own brief childhood

was sad as a shroud, who prayed
for a dutiful priest as a son;
who will die too young.

But for now she stands
between these two departures;
three years old, dressed

in a stiff white frock,
frowning at the camera's
toy-box gloom.

Soon she will struggle
through a flicker-book of mothers
but here she is, caught

on a dark glass plate;
she holds the chair leg firmly
like a bishop's wooden staff,

and makes the long lip
her quick *mama* interprets
as sorrowing to come.

Youngest

The line stops with her,
the youngest of the girls,
their blonde *benjamine*.

Before her, four sisters
refract into adulthood,
their heavy skirts sway

-ing up to the altar, and she
stands on tiptoe to admire
love's enfolding moments.

She dreams young of making
her oblation—a petal, flaming high
in Christ's kaleidoscope.

An Offering *(i)*

Her older sister, Léonie,
had her own troubles

yet learned young
to sacrifice. Mama encouraged her
with corks in the kitchen drawer
—one for each victory over the self!

One day she approaches
Céline and Thérèse
in the garden, bearing
her basket of childish things.
I've finished with these,
she says. *Please help*
yourselves.

Céline fishes, primly,
and brings out a ribbon,
a button, a porcelain doll.
Thank you, she says,
after a pause.

Léonie turns to Thérèse
and what would you like?

Sunlight dapples the grass.

All of it, says Thérèse,
She stretches out her hands.
I'll take it all.

Twenty years later
when she was already
starting to die,
she remembered.

It made her smile.
I've never refused
what God offers, she wrote,
the scraps, the trials, the confines
of my tiny life;

the bitter pills,
the hours of emptiness,
the bad dreams,
the *pointes de feu*,

this basket of words in the night.

A Glass Full

Thérèse, aged six, sits at the table.
Her legs swing under the wooden chair.

She is troubled by God's grace,
and how one can be full of him

yet smaller than a doll's house. How
can it be fair, when some are saints,

but most are limited sinners?
In her hand, a white-petaled aster

warms and thins against her skin.
Pauline lifts a jug of water,

is teacher and mother, and pours
cool blessing into cup and tumbler;

liquid shimmers at the brim of each.
And which is fuller? Both, she answers,

unpeeling the flower from her palm
and slipping it into the smaller vessel,

where it settles in its little pool
as she wipes a spilled droplet away.

Photo 2 *1881*

Two demure daughters
pose in the studio; each
dressed in the latest style
from the *Conseiller Universel;*

behind them, a photographic
trompe-l'œil screen:
a large flat open window
and a fountain in a garden.

Céline's a proud twelve,
the swell of her hips
held by her dark frock's lines;
high neck, deep vee. Her arm

encircles eight-year-old Thérèse;
a child whose gaze meets
the lens; chin up, hair long
and fair, and in her hands

a woven jump-rope, held
in its twist of youth, as, soon,
she'll hold her habit's rosary
in the cloister garden

of Carmel's enclosure,
where the tall cross offers
its own play of mercy –
and she makes herself at home.

Photo 3 *February 1886*

At this subtle cusp –
when girlhood curves

into adolescence, she
is caught in a liminal cameo,

head just tilted upwards,
held in the stiff round collar

of her dress. Fair hair
cascades down her back.

She's smiling, as no doubt
instructed. And shy, perhaps,

to gaze at *Monsieur*'s lens,
she seeks the middle distance.

This is the portrait Mabille
distorted, pinching

her eyes together, calling her
slow, morbid, schizoid.

Céline retouched it too,
with brush and *gouache*,

seeking to restore her
little sister long since dead,

and dream with her again
in the belvedere: those days

prayer-quilted and spread
before them like the sky;

the golden ache of God; clouds
scudding under the sunset,

and all they knew of destiny
in one held breath.

Christmas Miracle *1896*
Papa the irascible
mutters his festive
fatigue at the need
for childish presents
stuffed in the slippers
at least, he spits,
it's the last time for this –
his thirteen-year old daughter
catches her breath
at his bitterness.

A dash for the stairs
and a gulped-down sob.
Wait a while,
Céline advises,
pray with me, she says.
But Thérèse is new
as a natal star
in the dark old sky
and an old man's ways
are the wrapping
for this, the giving
up of all she had

because of the call
of love over love.

Papa Picks a Flower

It's May, 1887. He listens
to his daughter; pats

her hand distractedly, then rises
like the old man he's become;

shuffles to the flowerbed
while Thérèse stays seated,

back straight, and soul straighter.
When he returns, he offers her

an aster, its little petals
and fragile roots

lifted entire from the family soil.
She takes the flower to press

between heavy covers. Soon
its skin becomes translucent,

its scent released into the paper;
the whole flower thins, transforms.

After nine years the roots break off.
She holds her pencil in one hand,

sketching a brief outline
of the white flower in the other.

Pranzini *First Child*

This is what she calls him,
the dashing murderer,
shackled unrepentant
in a Paris jail-house.

His face is grainy, grey,
in the pages of *La Croix*;
she traces her blessing,
lifts her smudged fingers

and pleads for a sign.
Days pass. She prays.
He is taken to the scaffold
and bows to the blade –

but not before begging
to kiss the crucifix.
The paper obliges
with news of this grace,

she folds its words
away in her heart;
her first confirmed adoption –
she is a mother now.

L'Ascenseur

Paris, 1887. Thérèse is there
with Papa and Céline,

on pilgrimage. This
is a worldly interlude,

The Louvre with its risk
of colour and flesh,

and afterwards the *Galeries*,
where Papa buys his daughters

Parisian raincoats, blue
and chic in the tinted glass.

Céline is drunk on art, sees
the blur of life around her

as a palette to be dipped in.
Thérèse thirsts for God;

she wants to be alone
in her poor heart's chamber.

Back at the hotel, the girls
take the elevator. Each

feels the pit of her
stomach lurch.

Céline imagines
that this is what love does;

Thérèse, as the lift ascends,
understands love.

Petition

The pilgrims wait in line,
now it has come to this:

the blessing of a thin old man
with white hair, in a white robe

sitting in for God. Each visitor
kneels and dares not speak;

at a sign, the choreography
of grace will usher them away.

Céline stands behind Thérèse;
pushes the small of her sister's back –

it's now, she whispers. *Speak.*
And so the teenage girl in black

petitions him against the rules;
that she may give herself to rules

of life so strict there would
be no more travel, no more men

and no one sitting in for them.
He cannot utter more than *if*

God wills it. But as the guards
lift her away, he notices

the flash of the sun in her eyes,
the gold flare under her lace.

Little Ball

She rolled with Pauline's image
of a blond, toddler god,

who takes his cheap toy up,
shakes it; pulses it away.

The bruised little ball
gathers dust in its corner.

Suddenly the *fort-da* deity
reaches out again,

only to lift and jab it through
with a sharpened stick –

it whispers *Child*; he
is pleased with his gift;

just as Thérèse is given
to think herself disgraced;

her playmate reels her back
and pierces her again.

Photo 4 *April 1888*

Madame Besnier takes the portrait
three short days before she enters –

she is fifteen, her tresses twined
up in a bun. Her blue dress hugs

her body in a way she will foreswear,
her hands are demure; her face bright.

Later, Céline will slim her spine
with artist's *gouache*—to an arch,

tighten her image
to sanctity's pattern

like and unlike the Thérèse she knew.
Thérèse herself looks straight ahead:

smiling—at the camera's *examen*
and the dark veil that surrounds it.

IN CARMEL

Escalier menant aux cellules

The staircase rears its mane in a wave
over the hallway, its slim door-lines
either side of a white recessional.

The photo captures time just as
the curve of stairs suggests a risen flux,
its wooden slats and bolts a hold

on the pure heart's moon-drawn surge.
Its dark rise is a nun's veil's cadence,
each whispered step an *Ave*,

and overhead, a wreath of silence
hovers like a ring of airborne birds
buoyant and buffeted in the shimmering sky.

Photo 6 *Novice, 1889*

She is just sixteen, and clings
to her pillar of faith,

plump as a duck, or a goose
stuffed with buttery prayers.

Papa delivers fish, wine,
fur-lined boots, to the convent turn

and the sisters question
(after their silent supper) how

such a child could ever learn
the art of suffering on her own.

Mother scolds her when she
drops her cloth, broom, fork –

forgets to drop her gaze,
rejoices at a play of light

on Mary's statue. Thérèse
kneels and kisses the floor.

Even now, she's working
on her heart's first draft,

her young soul proven
and rising like dough.

Snow

The snow she'd always loved –
delicate and white,
winter blossom, heavenly
host melting on the tongue;
each communion unique
and given freely—so
she dared to pray for snow
to mark her vows, prayed to be
given to the cold; resolved
to the filigree of soul-work –
dissolved at the ushering
of the sky's breath.

Réfectoire

Meals are twice daily;
soup or stew ladled
into plain bowls,
salt passed along
by a system of signs.
After murmured grace
twenty or so spoons
are lifted and lowered.
One sister foregoes her food,
ascends the pulpit, reads
the latest *circulaire* aloud,
Another does penance
prostrate on the flagstones.
Sometimes there is wine,
strong, French, and red:
a sip for every suffering soul.
They listen, sharing their silence
over a basket of broken bread.

Thérèse and Martha

Martha, white-veiled
sister, consigned

to convent drudgery,
the cold of the wash-house

the hen coop's stink,
fell just a little

for the Mother Prioress.
Most sisters did—

her regal features,
peremptory scolding,

a sudden, flashing smile
and you'd be hooked.

Thérèse, just sixteen,
knew herself

how sweet such crumbs
taste on dark days.

Still she took Martha
under her wing,

helped her wash
her heart until it shone

translucent, ready
to crack and hatch

a fledgling love,
astringent, pure,

and resilient
to doubt's black spot.

Sister St. Peter

The elderly nun
shakes her hourglass –
you, there, Sister,

let's get on with it.
Thérèse steps up,
and helps the hurting limbs

into a rhythm of sorts,
towards a refectory
forever receding.

She gets no thanks.
She is too quick, too young:
the cloister holds its breath.

Somewhere in her body
music plays; the fizz
of a waltz perhaps;

a ripple in the skin
of life beyond its walls.
The sky is inky blue.

The elderly nun
seated at last, struggles
with her cutlery,

so Thérèse slices
the bread and cheese,
and on impulse

turns her face
to Sister St Peter's,
and leans in for a kiss.

Fire

Fire is in short supply
in the Normandy convent:

cold showers, cold cells;
only the warming-room

to offer its two kind hours.
She suffers like the others,

but tries to hide its chill,
suppressing her shivers,

keeps her blue fingers
under the brown scapular.

The cold clarifies her gaze,
makes her will burn the more,

just as her vision becomes
acute in the long watch

before the silent sacrament.
A song flickers in her

heart's poor hearth, lights
the loose papers,

home-made holy cards,
the dry wit, the smile,

confidently kindling
all the fire of love's refrain.

Letter of Supplication

from Sister Marie of the Sacred Heart

Ah! This life is passing exile. Pray draw near:
your visits to the parlour are most cherished.

Soon we shall all be freed from prison walls!
Do bring the lettuce, none have flourished here,

we would be truly pleased to use it. Should
you find peonies, *Sœur* Thérèse would love

to have them. Simple beauty fills her heart.
Alas! What a painful distance from our home

is this poor life. What suffering. We have
finished the tonic from the red glass bottles.

A refill would be marvellous. And if
you bring corn-cockles, she will smile,

though you behind the grille can hardly tell
her pleasure, in these brief but sweet bouquets.

She loves the lilies; misses them. And says
that violets, asters, eglantines are as true

to her as holy poems. Please consider
a rose or two. I sit writing to you

as the light fades from our cell. My stream
of days will soon have soaked into the earth.

She loves each petal. Ah! Her little ways.

To Pick up a Pin

a glinting filament
fallen from its basket –
restored to usefulness

a mantle puddled
on the cloister floor
folded and soothed

a few pressed petals
sweetly placed; a
secretly made card,

an hour given to thought
of how a nothingness
can fill itself with light,

and a poem pressed
into the hand, gleaming
with love's intuition.

Writing Desk

Her first is a fine acquisition:
smooth blanched grain, a gift

for young Jeanne Fleuriot, who never
entered; it's as pristine as a novice.

She pens her first letters from Carmel,
slides the top aside, revealing

ink, a scraper, blotting paper,
folds her first poems,

tends her thoughts in silence.
1894: she gives it to Céline,

preparing her sister's cell;
a welcome gift. It's little used.

Thérèse creeps up to the attic,
chilled feet in clumsy sandals,

finds another *écritoire ancienne*,
smiles at its rejected roughness.

Now she works with heaviness,
splintered corners; one great split

rending the surface. It comes
to suit her suffering soul:

she pens her final memoirs
the last few poems, and

a *Credo*, in the ink of her own blood,
writing her heart out on dark wood.

Photo 8 *November 1894*

She emerges from her hidden years
(postulant at fifteen, novice

at sixteen, solemn profession
one year on)—is used

to the Rule; to denying herself
all pockets of warmth and ease; she

has wiped the brows of the fevered,
knelt at the deathbed of *Mère* Geneviève

whose last tear she preserves
on a torn cloth, near her heart.

Now Céline is here, and brings
her camera to immortalise

their fleeting forms; Thérèse's face
a distant sibling in the Darlot lens,

obscured by the craquelure of
Carmel's bare branches; listening,

intently, for the murmurs
of her Child. Hold still, says Céline,

for the span of a prayer, let me
capture you at last, little sister: you

who draw me on, and leave me
gasping for light at your side.

Little Carmelite

who took the blame for breakage
and gathered up the fragments,

who spun a poem from dust
and another out of night

who took her own short story
and wove a skein of life,

who knelt down in prayer until
her feet dreamt of stars;

who sat with the unfriended,
worked with the unloved,

made the Prioress's sister
as welcome as an angel;

reported daily headaches
to the point of mockery,

taught as she had loved
and became a living rule,

whose little world blossoms
under her sword's steel.

Photo 10 *Lourdes Courtyard, November 1894*

Céline disliked the habit,
claiming it bulky, unbecoming –

in previous decades a sign
of no vocation. But today she dons it,

ahead of her vows, stiff toque and veil
encasing her face, as though she's pressed

herself through a thick blank canvas.
Pauline holds the family reins,

Experience folds her into place,
great key and rosary beads hang down

from her compact body. Marie,
a little dreamy even here, is amused

by the tawny box her sister bids
them pose for. Marie de Gonzague

is the ghost at the gathering, erased
post-mortem, lingering still. Only

Thérèse, the group's pale centrepiece,
thinks to gaze beyond its frame,

waiting, perhaps, for the choir's bell,
its intricate set sound, where she

can sit in an oblivion of grace,
and fade, as the dusk delivers her

to the one word in her heart.

La Sainte Robe sans couture

The Holy Robe
without seam or stain
hovers in the heavens.

Two cherubs hold
a circlet of thorns
above the absent face.

Thérèse has traced
an artist's grid
onto the tiny card

intending to paint
the baby angels –
less by hand than heart.

Each angel bears
its pencilled cross
aloft, a method of grace;

she steadies her gaze
and lifts her little brush
to the altarpiece.

Tonsure

The sisters said that
at the monthly cropping

of each nun's hair beneath
wimple and veil, Thérèse

would ask to be shorn
on the crown, like a monk,

or a priest. She would
usually oblige her,

whichever sister was
tasked with the cutting.

Then Thérèse would smile, smooth
her hand over her scalp –

a secret sign. Toque
back on. Veil. Cloak:

she is a nun again.
And yet, how happily

she wore it, her
hidden ordination;

month after month
this renewal of vows,

full like the moon
in her tonsure of clouds.

The Warming Room

It is a prayer like any other,
this circle in the warming room,

the older sisters ease themselves
onto proud wooden chairs,

the middle-aged on meditation stools,
the young sit on their heels.

Fire flickers its brief respite
from the Normandy winters,

and twice a day, light talk
transfigures the bare walls.

Gossip is scotched out
as it could burn them,

but a friendly word,
family news, the latest

headline, or a new recruit,
enlivens. And for feast days,

the novices play-act,
inhabit sudden characters,

ad-lib their lines,
provoke unlikely laughter.

Thérèse makes her sisters
glow with their memories;

Ask her, Marie says,
to write down her life,

as an act of obedience.
Pauline obliges, and Thérèse

takes on the task, weaving
the story of her soul,

the lines of her small world
a prayer like any other.

Rattled

A tiny scrape
of nail on tooth
distracts her
from her silence;

it is vespers, and later
the scrape will turn
to an incessant *tick*
as vigil is kept

for Our Lady's eve.
Thérèse kneels;
knots together
her own desire

to turn and hiss
at this sister beside her;
God knows prayer
is elusive enough

without the wretched snag
of sound. The clicking

itches through her resolve,
a mouse scratching

at the soul's low door.
She breathes it down,
inhales the wax and wane
of the night. But nothing

comes of intercession,
so Thérèse in poverty
offers the song
of nail on tooth.

It silvers the dark
as a grace note gleams
over the pause
between heaven and earth.

Photo II *1895*

She always said she would die
with weapons in hand, and here

she's dressed for the battle, stepping
in for the warrior maid of France –

drawn sword in her right hand,
banner in her left; unfurled,

the flag proclaims *Jesu, Maria.*
A hint of silver spurs. At her side

the courtyard shrine of Our Lady
of Providence, whose slender form

has blessed the sisters, curing them
of ulcers, sickness, sadnesses –

Thérèse-as-Joan stands sentinel
over their blessed mother;

She has made her vows.
She waits without word from her King.

Photo 13 *Joan of Arc in Her Prison*

It's spring, 1895. Thérèse
in the role of Joan, is chained

to the sacristy courtyard's
high brick wall. There is no sky.

She is dressed for the part –
full gown marked with *fleurs-*

de-lis; her long hair flows
—though not in fact her own –

her wrists are shackled,
her head's in her hand.

Thérèse-as-Joan imprisoned,
awaiting her final trial,

her costume flammable,
her heart even more so,

every prayer is so much straw
strewn on the hardened earth.

The camera's grace holds her
to this icon of her mission

(the story-arc she'll follow to the end,
the act of love she's written);

sunlight gleams on the water jar
and the brief lines by her side.

Handwriting

Her *little mother*, Pauline,
oversaw her learning,

from behind the convent grille
she fed her on pictures

and fibreless, sugary stories.
Six years later, Thérèse came in,

and Pauline kept an eye
on her deportment –

the incline of her head at prayer;
the angle of her script.

Lean your words to the right,
she told her. *Follow my bars and loops.*

Thérèse obeyed. Even in drafting
her plays where devils rattled

at their cages, and Joan of Arc
was chained in her dark prison –

she forced her lines to curtsey. Only
near the end, Pauline relinquished

her fussy instruction. *Write*
as you long to. So then the letters

of her sister's hand soared skywards,
stretching up in uttered confidence

that God would take her at her word
and lift her even higher.

Photo 17
Recreation in the Alley of the Chestnut Trees, 1895

In summer they carry
their baskets of work
into the chestnut alley,

where sunshine warms their faces,
hands, habits; and twice
a day they get an hour to chat

as they sew, draw, paint,
or cut tough bread into chunks
for the morning soup.

Some look at the camera in its box,
as the slow photo's taken,
their eyes meet ours across

more than a hundred sepia years
and they darn and daub, and smile
at long-gone comments.

Thérèse stands at the back,
an artist's palette in her hand,
circling her right arm around

the Infant Jesus
entrusted to her care;
instinctively maternal in the midst

of all the older women.
Her gaze extends beyond
the photo's edge. She's twenty-two,

has two years to live,
and the whole stumbling world
to gather up and love.

Photo 20
Hourglass (i), 1895

She is almost the youngest. Her face
retains an adolescent plumpness

as she stands with the four
novice nuns she is training
for decades of self-sacrifice.

Marie of the Trinity's crumpled veil
resembles a Flemish lady's portrait;
she is pretty, and almost a friend.

Martha leans to her *de facto* mistress
loyal as a greyhound, since Thérèse
has pulled her away from old sins.

Marie-Madeleine du Saint-Sacrament
kneels, with slim face and sharp eyes.
She struggles to trust even herself.

Céline stands apart, as if sailing
a little late from port, pulled
behind by the century's sepia,

compelled, nonetheless
to mark this day with art.
Thérèse is their hub of grace,

she clutches an hourglass:
her life's soft sift runs through it,
swift into God's large palm.

Hourglass *(ii)*

In the photo she clutches an hourglass;
her fingers pale against the brown
of her habit; the timer's wooden frame.
The glass curves in at the centre, flares
to a perfect rounded base; seconds
sift through its narrow waist and pool
below. Thirty minutes—then
the whole is turned, and time begins again.
And so the round of days, the watch
of self, the grace each moment can afford;
she knows herself to be a grain of sand,
small; self-spending; continually poured.

On the Door

Why did she carve his Name
on the inside of the door?
He is my only love, she wrote,
– mon unique amour,
as though it were a school desk
and she a teenage lover;
as though she were a prisoner
and he, elsewhere, another –
or that this place – this little cell,
was where she felt him most,
and set to make remembrance
in the world, of being his host.

Laundry

These are hard days:
the sodden sheets, robes, scapulars
are scrubbed with salt and ash

and now need rinsing,
rolling, beating, rinsing again,
in the convent's wash-house pool.

Every nun is needed; they jostle
each other at the water's edge,
grip their wooden paddles,

plunge their hands into the cold.
The heavy fabrics billow and contract;
their fingers burn and freeze.

To keep their spirits up, they sing,
rounds and home-made verses,
pummelling, wringing in rhythm –

then Sister Marie-Joseph
splashes Thérèse, her neighbour,
with sour grey water. She

closes her eyes too briefly
to be noticed. When she opens them,
they shine – on Marie-Joseph,

and her lilting hymn, the blue-white
skin of the sisters' wrists, the dim
reflections of the pool – on everything.

Photo 35 *Hay Making, June 1896*

The sun pours down
its grace like honey;

Céline and Marie squint,
smiling, in its light.

Martha stands alone,
discovered by joy.

Marie de Gonzague leans
on the years of her calling.

Thérèse is here, blurred,
her heavy fork held up,

ready to lift and gather
the summer-fresh hay.

Straw for stuffing mattresses;
fat bed-barrels, one per cell,

set to receive in secret
the imprint of a woman,

be moulded with her shape,
the turns of her sleep

while the seasons roll on,
and night after lucid night

each sister dreams of heaven
as a meadow in the sun.

Hebdomadaire

To sing seven by seven –
to lead each office with your call,
to cast its Latin as a silver thread
unspooling over the bowed heads
of sisters who respond like doves –
to murmur the graces of night,
to stand like a priest in the morning,
hold sunlight in your hands, your mouth,
to close your eyes in its warmth
to celebrate your weakness.

Little Things

The little water stoup by the cell door,
the holy cards stowed in a little box,
the little basket holding sewing work,
the little heated brick to warm the bed.

The little candleholder made of tin,
the little inkwell and the copybooks,
the jug, the facecloth and the little comb,
the little pencil and the little brush.

A little touch—at night a little smile,
a little way of love throughout all time.

Photo 29 *March 1896*

She sits for a formal portrait
against the cloister pillar;

mantle over long black veil,
half-squinting at the sun.

In her right hand she holds
The mission of Su-Tchuen,

—a gift from Father Roulland.
Her other holds a scroll,

on which she's written *I would give
a thousand lives to save a soul –*

The light makes her look older
than her twenty-three years.

Perhaps she is hungry; meals
are sparse in number, and

she never takes her fill, Thérèse,
six years professed, and only one

to live (already the doubts crowd in).
The cloister's arch recedes

behind her; and she wonders
what she can give in return,

self-sealed as she is, in her heart's
dry chambers; willing to burn.

Cellule de Thérèse

Her last cell is just like her first:
polished wooden walls and floor,
a mattress stuffed with hay and layered
with a rough brown blanket;
a small, low table for her little lamp;
her wicker basket; needles, scissors;
thimble. Prayer-books. *Écritoire.*

Here she coughs blood in the dark,
(the fog invading her), takes half
an hour to unpin her mantle, fumbles
with belt and rosary; trembles herself
to sleep. And then one bright dream

like a night-blooming cereus:
foundress Mother Anne, who says
God loves you, as she covers her up
with her own great shining veil.

Boat

He sleeps on in her boat,
this Jesus who persists

in silence. Faith is artless
as the wobbling mosaic

of moonlight on the water
which offers her its grace

but renders only the cold
silk shock of nothing.

Her hands are always empty,
her sail a thin gauze,

while the water is becalmed
and the clouds mass overhead.

Photo 40 *Sacristans*

It's 1896, an overcast day
in the sacristy courtyard:

they know she is ill, so ask
for a family photograph.

Marie and Pauline
describe and press

small discs of white
from the wheat-flour sheets.

Cousin Marie kneels in front,
bright in her novice's veil,

she pours wine from a jug,
her two hands aloft.

Céline, having posed
the whole tableau,

places herself centre-bench,
circling the cutters

for the great altar breads
so each one bears

a Christ forever crucified.
She looks to her right:

Thérèse at the far side
stands behind a table.

The chalice gleams there.
Over it she holds a single host,

keeping herself steady
for the plate's light and shade

like a priest, or a doctor
willing to solve love's cage.

Projection

She writes to Diana in faith,
not knowing the girl is a fake,

abused into existence
at Taxil's fiddling hand.

Diana, Palladian escapee;
Diana the convert from rottenness,

someone who might respond
to a gentling of her world,

self-birthed, young, and tender,
someone who might be a friend.

* * *

Send your photograph, says Mère Agnès,

*the costume with the fleurs-de-lis,
and you as enchained warrior.*

She pastes the citrate strip
onto a holy card and blesses it.

* * *

I see in you myself, had I
another occurrence in this world,

I see divinity in you, lifting
your heart from its poor prison,

gracing you your lines,
the lilt of a different song,

something that gathers
and echoes recursively,

to—*listen*—high harmonics
from a perfect curve of glass.

* * *

I thank you for your words,
the image of you, sword in hand,

all the cuts I've suffered
wither to nothing at your intercession.

* * *

Meanwhile, there is blood,
spilled from the gullet, shed in secret,

all the rigours of Lent
with its purpling of the light,

dreams that cell-bound sisters
dare not tell each other;

one of a red-edged doorway
to which Thérèse is called,

and told to make herself glorious
after her father's orders.

* * *

It's not that I never had it,
the propensity to sin,

but that I knew, had I committed
the senseless worst, I still could run

into her arms and be lifted up
over the ruptured world.

* * *

There is a bright assumption
in the patrons we invoke;

unsheathing strength
from a life accomplished,

we make our holy pictures;
raise an image up as though

the shell of it might whisper
the ocean's reassurance.

* * *

I shivered after the clouds
had effaced all trace of love;

But I kept to my song,
fashioning lyrics of what

I long to believe, as strongly
as if I were bathed in the sun –

* * *

Thérèse, in this last season,
senses her soul willing

to flow back to the world;
become part of life's pattern,

beyond the body's walls and
the bricks that block the sun –

but first there is stripping,
and mocking, Thérèse

displayed in an atheist's show,
as a dressed-up, gullible *Jeanne d'Arc*,

by sleek-haired Taxil, who
is Diana, who is the fraudster,

who unwittingly becomes
her brother at the sinner's table

as she shines around him,
as large as a map of the world,

sending out her letters
from a single point of light.

Little Lamp

Little lamp, whose wick
she pulls up with a pin

flickers in the dark night,
is a little spark

in which she kindles
a few more little words,

little glass inkwell
in which she spits

to make the blackness
last a little longer

lets her write
her little scraps of faith

traced with ink and blood
in the dark June nights.

Brother

1896. Pauline approaches her
with an unusual favour. *Here,*

she says, *I have found you a brother,*
in need of your prayers, and the other

lovely gift you have, of words. Thérèse
is not sure how she can answer to this

but sits in her cell with a pen
and a letter is written. Later,

She sends him poems, a photograph,
he writes of the path on which he stumbles,

she offers her response: *just keep on trying.*
Eventually, she tells him she is dying.

He fears that once in heaven she will see
how greatly he's sinned. But she

imagines her hands clasped warm in his
as he gives her his blessing.

On her request he sends her
a few brown strands of hair;

she holds their sparse grace,
released from the paper's fold,

knowing her breath and the breeze
from the sickroom window

could disperse them in a second,
and lets them rest beside her.

Liquidity

Coffee for the priest,
hot and black in a silver pot;
his wisdom is thick with its flavour
in the dim confessional.

Cider from the cellar,
drawn from barrel to bottle,
accompanying the midday soup
in a sequence of crisp sips.

White wine as a gift, from
one of the novice's fathers –
he spoils her, they say,
but none refuse a glass.

Red wine is rare, like a kiss,
it enriches the blood; is
offered at Mass, and transforms;
salve for the bitterest tasks.

Water in a humble jug.
No gulping. And milk,

which she never could stand.
Finally, a wretched medicine,

poured like a cordial, bright
in the daylight, sharp
as a heartbreak—she takes it,
and swallows down the night.

Holy Face

At seven, she sees a stranger
walking through the garden –

his face concealed
behind a shining cloth.

At seventeen, her *Papa* sinks
into insanity, pulling his napkin

over his features; ashamed,
perhaps, at what he's become.

Already a nun, she weeps
at Isaiah's Suffering Servant,

and joins the name
of the Holy Face to hers.

Two months before her death
she poses for the camera

holding her icons—the Child
and the Face—over her heart.

After her death, another photo,
her eyes shut, her lips

in the slightest of smiles,
leaving a lasting imprint

as she slips, light as a girl,
beyond the final veil.

Photo 43 *July 1897*

Thérèse is softly blurred, as though
– a second out of synch –

she has already started
her steps into eternity,

the atoms of her mortal body
beginning to phase-shift

away from the white-veiled group
of novices she loved.

Her face, in pain-laced effort
looks down at her last summer;

her right arm is raised,
waist-high, her small fist

clenched in final strength.
In it are soft rose petals,

and at her feet more.
Céline, Marie, and Martha,

and Marie-Madeleine,
aware of the camera's work

and their sister's slow departure,
form their frame of sadness.

This is the last shot standing
and in it she's falling

through hours like clouds
and scattering evening flowers

soft as kisses, lost
as drops of rain received

by the humble earth; as dear
as the ragged breath of the dying;

this confetti is her testament,
falling onto and somehow beyond

the cold stone blocks
at the foot of the cross.

The Agonies of Saints

The fashion then was pain. And pain was fashioned
by practicing the agonies of saints.

Often at dinner time, a *circulaire*, recounting
the final words, looks, gestures of a sister

before she took her ticket and sank down
into her carriage for the final stop;

or else the story of a blessed martyr
who chirruped on the scaffold like a bird

longing for flight, all dizzy for its blue
(the bacillus will take its victims too).

The doctor's like a shadow at the door,
threatening to block your exit from this life,

his medicine's a bitter ballast. *Pointes
de feu* at least adjust the soul to suffer

a tantalising bite of what's to come:
beautiful death, the final work of art:

a body hollowed from the inside out,
your gaze aflame. The casting off of doubt.

An Offering *(ii)*

But am I suffering well?
All through the long
months of her dying

her struck lungs
coughed up cups of blood,
the body's offering

to a god who burned
her heart to sheer flame,
her soul to a dark

ash-pit, where nothing
grinned its ghastly welcome.
The ache in her sides,

the exhaustion with which
she dragged herself
up the stairs to her cell;

the cracked, lost voice. Is
this suffering well?
To be wracked, that's

anyone's fate—good
thief and bad—but to
hold the pain up, or its

shadowy twin, despair,
as a gift, a little bird,
as bread—to accept

the twisted gut and breath,
to offer each staggering step –
all this she does,

for a God she cannot see,
who surely knows
she's nothing left to give him

save this last cup filled
to the brim, from the depths
of the suffering well.

Photo 44 *August 1897*

They wheel her into the cloister
for the last time, for a visit

to the Blessed Sacrament
she can't consume.

She's in her bed; she turns
her thinned-down face

to the side, ever obedient
to Céline's request.

She has a month to live – in which
the gangrene and tubercles

shred her body to a rag;
the blood comes up in clots,

her lungs fail. Each breath's
a stab in the guts. She drops

a few rose petals on her cross,
utters simple words which slip

into her sisters' notebooks.
I will come back, she promises.

The little cap and cloak blend
into the pillow. Her eyes,

once brilliantly clear,
are opaque black beads.

Her lips press together,
as though to stop a cry –

but she does not look away.

Infirmary

The bed itself is veiled,
half-ship, half-grave; she

compares it to a harbour
where the launch is delayed,

and though she is only
twenty-four, she claims

she has always waited.
The pain bears down,

she turns her thoughts
to Christ in his garden,

and asks for relief
to be taken away.

Daylight ebbs. They
bring a blessed candle.

Her body's tethers
loosen in black water.

Morphine

Pain comes in bands,
remains as bruises,
is sharp, dull,
tender, a scar,
an ache,
a loss –

and what used to be
twice-weekly discipline
admitted to the self –
whips to the back
over exposed shoulders –

is now an inner
condition of torment –
each breath
flogging the lungs –
it is too much.

Dr. de Cornière prescribes
morphine hydrochloride
mixed with sulfate,

a little cocaine,
giving her a few more weeks
of agony, and words.

The Prioress balks
at his injections:
shameful for a Carmelite,
whose work is pain,
its distilled essence
offered at Christ's feet.

And so she's left
on the rack of it,
with Marie and Céline
slipping her spoonfuls
of opiate syrup

and praying to take
the sin of pain's relief
onto themselves.

The Cross

Because she couldn't breathe –
was wracked with breath's lack,
too weak to raise herself,

Marie and Céline have lifted her
half-up from the bed, her
hurting arms spread and held

about their robed shoulders.
Tipped forward, she hangs
on the cross of herself,

as the night light flickers;
the last speck of sand has run
from the hourglass's lung.

She is heavy as a world,
a dying sun. But Céline –
unready still – flings out her hand

to force the air to move again; force
the sickroom's minutes back
into their fragile cycle,

and so they ease her down,
and she offers up their love.

Entering Life

she who had lived so little
breathed out her soul

like gold dust, having told
how much she loved

and now there was nothing
but starlight

a wide-open window
a wide-open sky

Photo 46 *1897*

October. It's over.
Thérèse seems to sleep,

as though she has closed
her eyes in final prayer,

relaxing at last into God's arms.
They have washed her

and robed her, fastened
her mantle with its wooden *tibi*,

pressed the circlet of white roses
over her veiled head, wound

the rosary about her hands.
Crucifix. Lilies. The martyr's palm.

Céline, perhaps, has gently
smoothed the final pain away.

She senses, as the camera
makes its memorial – light

and shadow silvering the glass –
that something important

is somehow beginning –
and when they take Thérèse away

Céline feels her absence
soft about the heart,

like the dawn rivering
through an unlocked gate.

AFTERWARDS

On the Roof *1901*

The sisters are up high
on the convent roof, between
cloister and garden. The sky
all around them is grey, empty
of ornament; just as they
have emerged from their century
into the unknown twentieth.

Her novices have aged –
Marie of the Eucharist is stiller,
and a little stooped, and sadder.
Marie of the Trinity has thickened
with the work that follows loss.

They stand together, those who
still live, have all lived through
Thérèse's sweetness and her agony,
have seen her words committed
into print and taken flight.

Whether she came up here herself,
aged, say, nineteen or twenty,
to breathe, unsupervised, a little closer
to a heaven she could never visualise,

to let her vow of hiddenness
loosen its seal in the air's plenty,

to look down at the cloister walk,
watch her sisters move in line and

curve about their day, and feel
her heart twist in a captive love,

to see herself as a written slip,
a line of a prayer or a verse, light
enough to drift out to the world,

or beyond it—perhaps some know,
picture her even—while the camera
makes its record of the solemn group,
keeping her secret like a little gift.

Letters

She comes to them in letters,
a few, at first, like early leaves
cradled through the summer's

turn, their paper ivory-shy, *I
write to you because her death –*
they gather tidily in her desk.

Then more fly in; little birds
seeking shelter. *You, who knew
her, say a little prayer for me.*

Then more, with testimonies,
pleas for intercession, relics,
medals, something of her likeness;

war comes, but still they flutter,
missives from mud-spattered hearts,
craving a little sweetness

in the midst of dissolution. Her
sisters sit in the garden, surrounded
by breathing letters that nestle

in the grounds of grief's castle.
She is the bud and stem of them all,
as they settle like petals.

The Very Sweet Scent of Heliotropes

It is there when she passes –
the little statue that Thérèse would tend,
the pink of his cheeks and tunic

once painted by her hand, releases
the scent like honey, adrift
on the afternoon breeze. Martha stands

warm with the sunlight touching
her face, his infant feet. She looks
for the bunch of petals, stepping

up to the child, scanning the *prie-dieu*
– nothing. Still the sweetness.
She drops for a moment to her knees,

rises – there's the laundry still to sort –
touches his face on impulse,
then walks on, cradling the scent

in her mind, like a childhood song.
Later she tells Mother Agnès,
a very sweet smell. The Prioress goes

to see for herself, her great cream cloak
a rippling moon in the dark. Inhaling,
she nods, and offers a soft, brief smile.

Eleven years, and at last this gift.
She whispers, *little sister,*
How we miss you.

The night sky is silent.
The cloister stretches two dark arms
beyond the brink of grief.

Gisant
La Chapelle de la Châsse

She lives in others' dreams
in the long years since her death

and here to house
her ribs' frail rigging,

the skull, neck, pelvis,
bones of leg and arm,

Céline has commissioned
a wax Thérèse, who lies

like a queen on her bed
with shining, shut-eyed face,

hands artfully releasing
a static gush of roses

that never reach the ground.
Marble angels shield her

like sugar statues, ready
to melt in adoration. She's

robed in rich cloth here –
silk, gold thread, fine linen,

a Sleeping Beauty, waiting
to be woken from this fake

assumption, by her Prince
for whom she gave her breath –

a breath that's flown beyond
the dreamer, the glass box,

leaving the hollow doll,
and the quiet bones inside.

Aux Roses

The top note is sweetness:
a quick hit of violets, but then
the strain of saccharine additives,

too much, already, for some.
Its blend has been revised
to suit more modern tastes;

back to the natural, the hint
of root and earth within the floral.
In the *sillage* is the scent

of roses, by which she is best known.
The rose oil calms the soul,
heals the heart. Warms the skin.

Below its velvet touch, though,
is the tang of blood, as befits
a woman's body: faith's flow

with all its clots and guts. Then,
something substantial again:
the structured gleam of metal,

an unsheathed sword-flash at
the battle ground. A base of soul
endures, infused with iron.

Reliquary
Lisieux Basilica

The flesh has melted away;
the muscles, veins, and skin,

and lifted from her body
are the two slim bones

of the forearm. Radius, ulna:
held in delicate suspension,

in their glass capsule, tender
little boat of stripped-back grace.

The bones that armed her –
and through which she wrote

and painted; raked, polished,
pummelled at the wash house;

offered hours of daily prayer;
embraced her sisters, doubt, darkness.

She once called her body
an envelope. Here is the fold

of the bone into its missing joint;
the soul has slipped out, unfurled,

leaving the forearm to gather up
the stranded and unformed,

and sheltering them, say
I was only young, I loved, grew

into and through the life I had,
and this is addressed to you.

Parallel

Imagine had the junctions slipped:
the waves of 1890s flu averted,
and a young nun made to accept

an extra blanket, responsible doctors
helping the soul settle into its skin.
Imagine her life unfolding, instead of

her cult; imagine her living through wars,
and writing, as the Carmel's Prioress,
the story of her soul. Merton, perhaps,

writing in turn to her; the two friends
plaiting together spark and wisdom,
taking on joint firewatch of the world.

And in this cosmos, my converted father,
with his wife and baby daughter
visiting Lisieux for her blessing;

imagine her frail frame – ninety-four,
at the far edge of the body, offering
love as dry and light as a leaf,

(slipping her hand through the gaps in the grille)
and softly tapping a weeks-old infant
fresh from creation, smelling of petals

and blood, and sensing hard-won heaven,
as my cloudy eyes look upwards,
meeting her own.

Patron

Aviators,
florists,
France,

those suffering illness,
or the early loss of parents;

priests in their loneliness,

sisters,
criminals,

those lost to faith, who
wonder how they got here:
here at the table of sinners
where there's no wine.

Children,
the fallen and bruised,
the confused,
those still waiting
for their mission

those with a burning
heart, throat, gut;
those at the fulcrum,

the youngest,
the smallest,
the febrile
the arid,

the too late,
the too soon;

all the wounded soldiers,
heavy-hearted,
leaden-footed,
migraine-ridden,
doubt-stricken,

anyone who asks for her,
sensing the still point in her soul,

anyone who comes across her
craving sweetness,
craving answers,

anyone who longs for
a smile from the half-open door:

she will be your sister,
with a shield, and a sword,
a rose,
and a whispered word.

The Antechoir

Last night I dreamt I was there,
in the antechoir, the space between

cloister and chapel, movement
and pure prayer. A waiting room –

where the sisters gather in pairs,
cream cloaks over workaday habits,

blinking the sleep from their eyes,
or the day from their minds. I was

alone, barefoot on the wooden floor
and I sensed her presence there;

Thérèse, not novice-young, nor yet
in solemn crowned repose,

but waiting in this place as though
to welcome them with a shaft of grace—

the drift of little souls she would lift up
against the window filled with light.

ACKNOWLEDGEMENTS

'Lourdes Courtyard' and *Hebdomadaire* first appeared in *Stride*.

'*Gisant: La Chapelle de la Châsse*' first appeared in *The Merton Journal*.

'On the Door' and 'Snow' first appeared in *The Windhover*.

'Novice' first appeared in *Ink, Sweat & Tears*.

'Laundry, 1895' and 'Thérèse and Martha, 1896' first appeared in *Psaltery & Lyre*.

'*Aux Roses*' first appeared in *Little Rose Magazine*.

'*L'Ascenseur*', 'April 1888', 'Brother', 'An Offering ii', 'On the Roof' first appeared in *Saint Katherine Review*.

'A Glass Full', 'To Pick up a Pin', 'Hourglass (ii)', 'Sister St. Peter', 'Handwriting', 'Little Lamp', 'Rattled' and 'The Antechoir' first appeared in *Soul-Lit*.

'Parallel' first appeared in *The Merton Seasonal*.

'Photo 13: Joan of Arc in her Prison' first appeared in *America*.

'Photo 8: November 1894' first appeared in *Marble*.

RESOURCES

There are many resources on Thérèse for those interested.

I highly recommend the archive web pages of the Carmel of Lisieux: http://www.archives-carmel-lisieux.fr/english/carmel/index.php/accueil-home
  This website contains photographs (all the photographs cited in this collection and more) and the full text of Thérèse's autobiographical manuscripts, her letters, poems, plays, and more.

The website *Thérèse of Lisieux: A Gateway* is also very informative: http://www.thereseoflisieux.org/

Books on Thérèse are also numerous. The following are good, and there are many others:

Edmonson, Robert J., cj, trans. *The Complete Thérèse of Lisieux.* Brewster, MA: Paraclete Press, 2009.

Görres, Ida Friederike. *The Hidden Face: A study of St. Thérèse of Lisieux* [English edition trans. Richard and Clara Winston] [New ed.]. San Francisco: Ignatius Press, 2003.

Kochiss, Joseph P. *A Companion to Saint Thérèse of Lisieux: Her Life and Work & The People and Places in Her Story.* Brooklyn, NY: Angelico Press, 2014.

Moorcroft, Jennifer. *Saint Thérèse of Lisieux and Her Sisters.* Leominster, UK: Gracewing, 2003.

Nevin, Thomas R. *Thérèse of Lisieux: God's Gentle Warrior.* Oxford, UK: Oxford University Press, 2006.

Nevin, Thomas R. *The Last Years of Saint Thérèse: Doubt and Darkness, 1895-1897.* New York: Oxford University Press, 2013.

Udris John. *Holy Daring: The Fearless Trust of Saint Thérèse of Lisieux.* Leominster, UK: Gracewing, 1997.

ABOUT PARACLETE PRESS

WHO WE ARE

As the publishing arm of the Community of Jesus, Paraclete Press presents a full expression of Christian belief and practice—from Catholic to Evangelical, from Protestant to Orthodox, reflecting the ecumenical charism of the Community and its dedication to sacred music, the fine arts, and the written word. We publish books, recordings, sheet music, and video/DVDs that nourish the vibrant life of the church and its people.

WHAT WE ARE DOING

Books

PARACLETE PRESS BOOKS show the richness and depth of what it means to be Christian. While Benedictine spirituality is at the heart of who we are and all that we do, our books reflect the Christian experience across many cultures, time periods, and houses of worship.

We have many series, including *Paraclete Essentials*; *Paraclete Fiction*; *Paraclete Poetry*; *Paraclete Giants*; and for children and adults, *All God's Creatures*, books about animals and faith; and *San Damiano Books*, focusing on Franciscan spirituality. Others include *Voices from the Monastery* (men and women monastics writing about living a spiritual life today), *Active Prayer*, and new for young readers: *The Pope's Cat*. We also specialize in gift books for children on the occasions of Baptism and First Communion, as well as other important times in a child's life, and books that bring creativity and liveliness to any adult spiritual life.

The MOUNT TABOR BOOKS series focuses on the arts and literature as well as liturgical worship and spirituality; it was created in conjunction with the Mount Tabor Ecumenical Centre for Art and Spirituality in Barga, Italy.

Music

PARACLETE PRESS DISTRIBUTES RECORDINGS of the internationally acclaimed choir *Gloriæ Dei Cantores*, the *Gloriæ Dei Cantores Schola*, and the other instrumental artists of the *Arts Empowering Life Foundation*.

PARACLETE PRESS IS THE EXCLUSIVE NORTH AMERICAN DISTRIBUTOR for the Gregorian chant recordings from St. Peter's Abbey in Solesmes, France. Paraclete also carries all of the Solesmes chant publications for Mass and the Divine Office, as well as their academic research publications.

In addition, PARACLETE PRESS SHEET MUSIC publishes the work of today's finest composers of sacred choral music, annually reviewing over 1,000 works and releasing between 40 and 60 works for both choir and organ.

Video

Our video/DVDs offer spiritual help, healing, and biblical guidance for a broad range of life issues including grief and loss, marriage, forgiveness, facing death, understanding suicide, bullying, addictions, Alzheimer's, and Christian formation.

Learn more about us at our website:
www.paracletepress.com
or phone us toll-free at 1.800.451.5006

SCAN
TO
READ

YOU MAY ALSO BE INTERESTED IN...

This Far: Poems
Kathleen O'Toole
ISBN 978-1-64060-262-5
$19 | Trade paperback

Wing Over Wing: Poems
Julie Cadwallader Staub

ISBN 978-1-64060-000-3
$19 | Trade paperback

Still Pilgrim: Poems
Angela Alaimo O'Donnell

ISBN 978-1-61261-864-7
$18 | Trade paperback

The Story of a Soul
A New Translation

Thérèse of Lisieux

TRANSLATED BY
Robert J. Edmonson, CJ

ISBN 978-1-55725-487-0
$16.99 | Trade paperback

Available at bookstores
Paraclete Press | 1-800-451-5006 | www.paracletepress.com